T0386725

365 Days of feel-good Art

This book belongs to:

365 Days of Feel-good Art

FOR SELF-CARE AND JOY, EVERY DAY OF THE YEAR

LORNA SCOBIE

quadrille

Welcome to 365 Days of Feel-good Art!

This is the fifth book in the *365 Days* series, and it felt more important than ever to create a book filled with specific tasks to encourage people to feel great. I have had many people reach out to me to say how creating art in their *365 Days* books has helped them manage anxiety and even pain. Art is a powerful tool and we're all equipped with the ability to use it.

Adding creativity into your daily life is a brilliant way to form a wonderful, feel-good habit that you can utilise throughout your life and share with others. Art can be a refuge when you are feeling low and a way to express and explore feelings – whether that's joy, sadness or something in between. It is also an opportunity to learn new skills and to observe the world around us with a sense of fascination and gratitude.

This book is for everyone – all ages and all skill levels. We can all use art as a vehicle to make us feel brilliant, and we are all creative beings. Sometimes there are things that get in the way of our creativity, and so this book is your safe space, designed to help you overcome any fears or self-doubt you might have about putting pen to paper. We can all feel intimidated by the blank pages in sketchbooks, so as well as there being a prompt to encourage your creativity every day of the year, I've also added some tips, and started off some of the activities. Most of us loved art as young children; perhaps we used it to tell stories about our life, to express how we felt and to play. It was fun, but also deeply calming. Sometimes that relationship with art can get lost over the years, so here is a chance for you to rediscover it.

There is no right or wrong, and there is no 'bad' art, so feel comfortable knowing this, and feel encouraged to embrace mistakes and to

experiment. Allow yourself to be playful, and adapt the activities in any way you like. You can use this book whenever you feel like you need a happiness hit. De-stress your mind with art rather than looking at a screen before bed, or try starting an activity after work to signal to yourself that now it's time to unwind and relax. Perhaps you prefer to draw in the mornings before reaching for your phone, or take your creative time on days off.

Find a space that allows you to create comfortably and happily. If you aren't feeling inspired, perhaps try a new location – this could be a different spot in your house, or you could venture out to a park or café. Your location is important, and it ideally needs to be somewhere you feel relaxed and able to express yourself. Be sure to create work for *yourself*, in any way that makes you happy. Be selfish about your art! Ask yourself: what do I want to create? What are my passions? What excites me? Try not to think about what you *should* be doing, or what you think others want you to do, but instead create art just for you. You'll see a lot of nature and sea in the examples I have added to this book, and this is because I personally feel very inspired and calm when surrounded by the natural world. But this might not be the same for you.

If a particular task isn't inspiring you – change it! You may want to take art beyond the book and continue your creative journey in sketchbooks, on canvas … on whatever you can find. Remember, this is your book, and you can use it in any way you like. The activities don't need to be completed in a particular order. You may enjoy some tasks more and these may spark further ideas – if you like something, explore it. Remember to focus on enjoying the process, and don't worry too much about the end result.

It's a fantastic idea to have art in your life every day, but we do live busy lives and that's not always possible. Be kind to yourself if you miss a few days, or even miss weeks or months. This book doesn't have to be completed in a year – it's there for you to pick up whenever you like. Similarly, if you'd like to do multiple activities in one day – that's great.

In this book I have included activities that encourage you to write down your thoughts. The **journal** pages are a space for free-writing, and you can use them in any way you like. This may not feel like doing art, but it can be very beneficial to think about how we are feeling, and it can also clear your mind so you are ready to embrace being more creative. Identifying how we feel can be extremely empowering.

There are also tasks that encourage you to **expand** your art. These are longer challenges which may take you outside of the book. You might need a bit more time to do them than the regular exercises, and it might be something you develop over a few weeks or even months. They will help deepen your creative journey and develop your own ideas and confidence.

Your creations can be personal, but if you do feel like sharing your artwork, do so with confidence! Use the hashtag **#365DaysOfFeelgoodArt** to share your art with the online community and see what else has been shared.

Activities Completed

1	2	3	4	5	6	7	8	9	10
11	12	13	14	15	16	17	18	19	20
21	22	23	24	25	26	27	28	29	30
31	32	33	34	35	36	37	38	39	40
41	42	43	44	45	46	47	48	49	50
51	52	53	54	55	56	57	58	59	60
61	62	63	64	65	66	67	68	69	70
71	72	73	74	75	76	77	78	79	80
81	82	83	84	85	86	87	88	89	90
91	92	93	94	95	96	97	98	99	100
101	102	103	104	105	106	107	108	109	110
111	112	113	114	115	116	117	118	119	120
121	122	123	124	125	126	127	128	129	130
131	132	133	134	135	136	137	138	139	140
141	142	143	144	145	146	147	148	149	150
151	152	153	154	155	156	157	158	159	160
161	162	163	164	165	166	167	168	169	170
171	172	173	174	175	176	177	178	179	180

181	182	183	184	185	186	187	188	189	190
191	192	193	194	195	196	197	198	199	200
201	202	203	204	205	206	207	208	209	210
211	212	213	214	215	216	217	218	219	220
221	222	223	224	225	226	227	228	229	230
231	232	233	234	235	236	237	238	239	240
241	242	243	244	245	246	247	248	249	250
251	252	253	254	255	256	257	258	259	260
261	262	263	264	265	266	267	268	269	270
271	272	273	274	275	276	277	278	279	280
281	282	283	284	285	286	287	288	289	290
291	292	293	294	295	296	297	298	299	300
301	302	303	304	305	306	307	308	309	310
311	312	313	314	315	316	317	318	319	320
321	322	323	324	325	326	327	328	329	330
331	332	333	334	335	336	337	338	339	340
341	342	343	344	345	346	347	348	349	350
351	352	353	354	355	356	357	358	359	360
361	362	363	364	365					

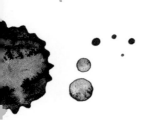

Tools and Materials

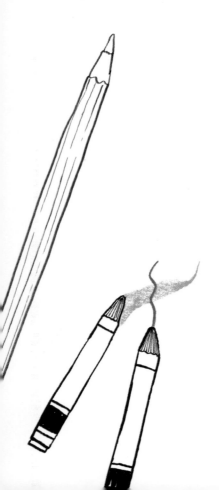

You can use any materials you like to complete this book – it's about finding what works for you. Explore materials you haven't used before, or use the exercises as opportunities to really enjoy the tools you love. Remember that the focus of this book is on your enjoyment of the tasks, and it's fine to try different materials to those suggested, if you'd like.

I feel most inspired to create when I get all my art materials out in front of me. Seeing lots of exciting materials and colours inspires me to experiment, and this leads to more energetic artwork.

Your materials don't need to be expensive. I have suggested a few of my favourite materials here, but these are by no means a necessity. Visit art shops for a range of options, and make use of the staff, who can offer excellent advice about different pens, pencils and paints to suit your needs. You could browse online for recommendations, or swap tips and discuss thoughts with friends and fellow creatives on social media.

Ink pens and paints might bleed through the page, so, if you are concerned that this might happen, you could prime the paper with **clear gesso** before you start your activity. This will form a layer between the paper and the material and will prevent bleeding – just be sure to allow plenty of time for the gesso to dry before you start.

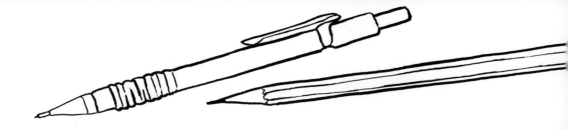

Pencils

Pencils and coloured pencils are a really versatile material. They are easy to use and are relatively mess-free. Pencils range in softness, most commonly from a 9B, which will create a very soft black line, to a 9H, which is extremely hard and creates a very sharp, light line. It might be useful to have a variety of pencils so you can experiment with the different effects they make. Try a 3B for shading and an H or 2H for crisp lines. If you are using pencils, you'll also need a good eraser and sharpener.

Mechanical pencils are also a great tool to have. Despite still containing a pencil lead, these feel more like a pen to hold as they are metal or plastic and often have a rubber grip for your fingers. I enjoy using the **Staedtler Mars Micro 0.5** and the **Pentel P205 0.5**. Mechanical pencils don't need sharpening, but you will need to buy extra lead refills for them. Make sure you choose the correct size of lead for your pencil (the mechanical pencil will say the lead it takes on its side).

My favourite coloured pencils are the **Staedtler Ergosoft** pencils, which are hard and create very solid, bright colour, and the **Caran d'Ache Supracolor** pencils, which have a softer lead and come in a huge range of colours. In art stores you can buy individual coloured pencils, so you can choose the perfect colour and style. I really enjoy the hues available in the **Faber-Castell Polychromos** range. Some coloured pencils are water soluble, so you can blend them with water and a paintbrush.

Fineliner pens

It's really useful to have a few black fineliner pens in your kit. These can be used for anything from jotting down notes and ideas, to quick sketches and adding details to artwork. There is a wide range of brands and nib sizes to choose from, so I recommend experimenting with the testers in an art store to see which you prefer. My favourites include the **Uni Pin Fine Line** pens, the **Sakura Pigma Micron** pens and the **Derwent Graphik Line Maker** pens.

Brush tip pens

These come in fantastic colours and can be great tools to draw with. I enjoy using the **Tombow Dual Brush Pens**, which are useful for colouring backgrounds or creating bold shapes and marks.

Watercolour paints

Sizes of watercolour palettes can vary. It can be convenient to have more colours in your palette, but the smaller sets are also great and you can mix colours to create a whole rainbow of hues. **Daler-Rowney** and **Winsor & Newton** both produce wonderfully vibrant colours. When you run out of a particular colour, you can even purchase individual replacements so your set of watercolours can last forever!

Paint brushes vary greatly too, and it's useful to have a range of brush sizes and shapes. Tips can be pointed, rounded and even square-ended, and each will produce a different effect. Experiment with different types. You'll also need a container for your water, which can be anything from a mug to an empty yoghurt pot, and some paper towel for blotting water off your brush. Make sure your brush is wet before you use it to pick up watercolour paint, and rinse it in the water before changing colour to keep colours clean. You could also try water brush pens. I like the **Pentel Aquash** water brush. These brushes come in a few sizes and can be filled with water, providing a useful alternative to a pot of water and paint brush when painting with watercolours.

Most palettes come with a space inside the lid to mix colours – a mixing palette. These can be revisited even when the paint has dried out, just by applying a bit of water from your brush. You can also buy additional mixing palettes if you prefer to have more space.

Wax pastels

These are a really fun material to use as they slide easily over paper and you can cover large areas quickly when using them on their sides. There is a great range of colours which can be bought individually or in sets, and you can even buy grips to stop your hands getting too messy! I like the **Caran d'Ache Neocolor II Aquarelle** pastels, which are water-soluble. Just add a little water to your wax pastel drawing using a brush or sponge for an interesting effect.

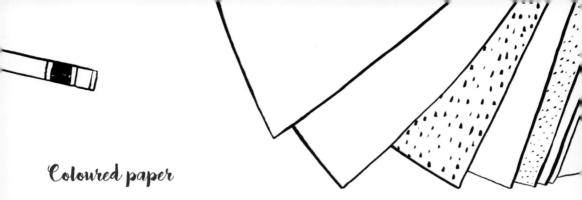

Coloured paper

Coloured paper is something you could buy as you go, and you can even use gift wrap or brown paper bags. It's a fantastic material to have in your kit as it's really useful for covering large surface areas and for creating collages. It can also be painted or coloured. Origami paper is handy as it is thin, easy to tear and cut, and often comes in a range of exciting colours.

Here are some other materials you may like to have in your art kit:

— **Sketchbooks:** Use these to continue your creative journey. They are a great place to experiment and record your ideas, and come in a huge range of sizes.

— **Clear gesso:** A primer to apply with a clean brush to paper or board to prevent materials from bleeding.

— **Acrylic paint:** Strong, bright colours, which dry quickly and can also be watered down. Be sure to wash brushes before the paint on them dries.

— **Gouache:** These are water-based paints, similar to watercolour but providing a more intense colour as they are more opaque. They dry quickly, but are great if you're interested in layering colours.

— **Scissors:** For collages and cutting paper.

— **Glue:** PVA or a gluestick can be used to stick down collages. Water down PVA to make it less gloopy.

— **Masking tape (low-tack sticky tape):** Handy for sticking things down quickly, easy to remove and draw on. Can also be used for straight lines; stick it down before you start, then peel off once finished to reveal a straight edge.

— **Tracing paper:** Use a bit of masking tape to stick this over drawings that are a bit messy.

— **Fixative spray:** Apply on top of completed artwork to prevent smudging.

— **Bulldog clips:** Useful for holding back other pages while you work on an activity.

1

A colour wheel can be used to see the relationship between colours and can also help you with choosing your palettes.

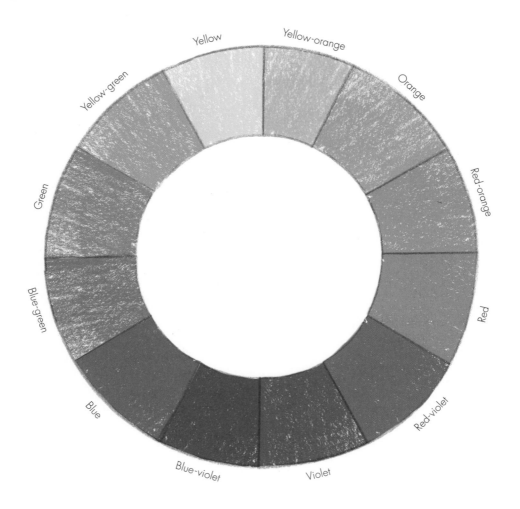

Analogous colours are groups of three or more colours next to each other on the wheel. These often form a harmonious palette. →

Complementary colours can be found opposite each other on the wheel, and these pairs will create striking contrasts within your work. →

Create your own colour wheel by adding in colours to the segments below. You can use any material you like, even coloured paper.

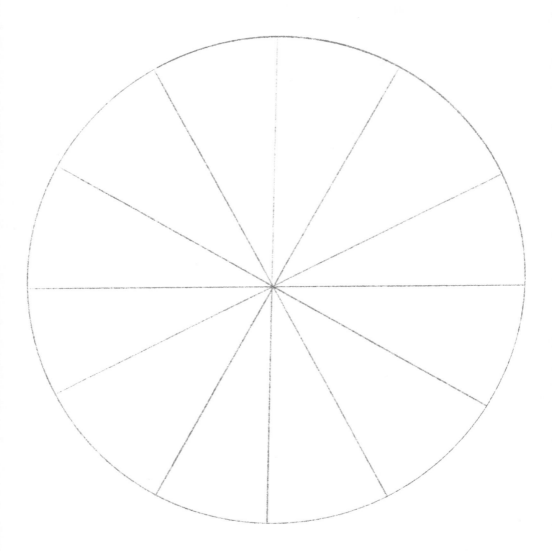

Tip: You may like to refer back to this colour wheel when you are completing other activities. You could even photocopy it and keep a copy with your art materials.

2

Design your own beach huts. They could be colourful and patterned. Perhaps there are people on the beach in front, and maybe you can see the sea too.

3 ———— Finger-painting can be a great way to get more comfortable with being a bit messy with your art supplies. Fill the page with finger-painted blobs and create an abstract piece of art.

Tip: Dip your fingertips into watercolour or watered-down acrylic paint. Making a mess can feel like a mistake, but with art, it's not! Go for it, and enjoy colour and chaos!

4 ———— Draw your reflection regularly over a period of a week or so. The drawings don't need to be large, so you could use the spaces below. You may like to spend just a few minutes on each one, or choose to take longer.

Tip: Concentrate on drawing what you see, rather than what you think you see.

Once you have completed the drawings, think about what positives you can take from this activity. Maybe you see a gradual improvement, or perhaps you approach the task more confidently each day.

5 ——— Explore blending colours. Use any materials you like and see how colours mix when they are combined. Painted colours might run into each other, and dry materials can be blended together on the page.

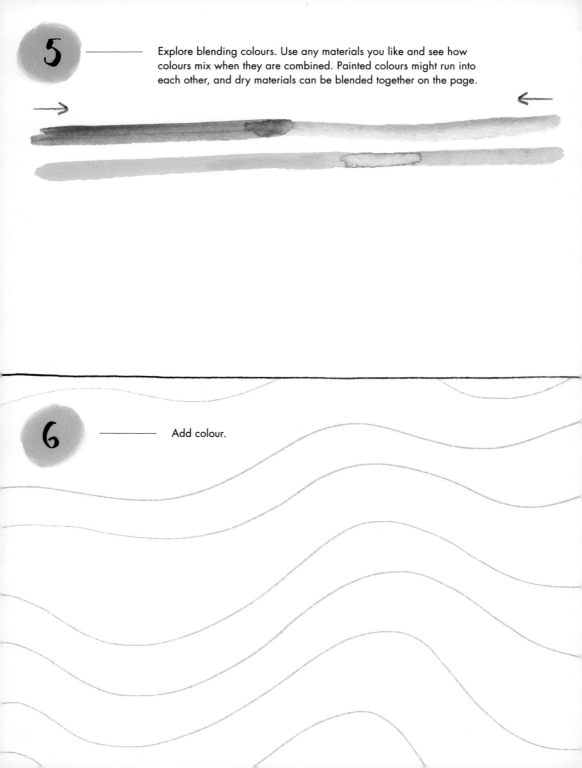

6 ——— Add colour.

7 ——— Here is a space for you to write down anything you like. It could be anything you feel grateful for, or positive about, or ideas for art!

8 ——————

Find a photograph or image from a magazine that makes you feel great. Stick it anywhere on this page and then draw the rest of the scene around it. The drawing doesn't have to be realistic, and you could just focus on extending the colours you see, using abstract shapes.

Tip: Use a glue stick or double-sided tape to stick in your image.

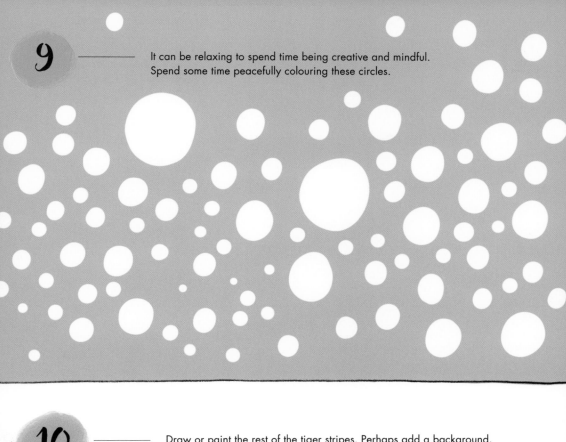

9 ———— It can be relaxing to spend time being creative and mindful. Spend some time peacefully colouring these circles.

10 ———— Draw or paint the rest of the tiger stripes. Perhaps add a background.

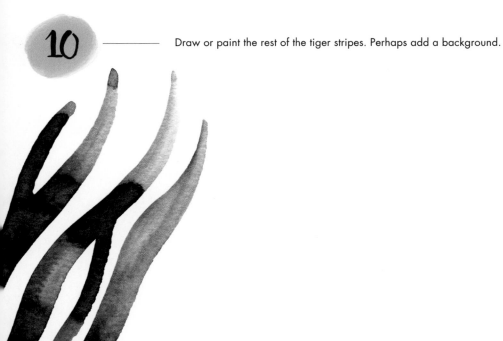

11 ——————— Draw a wild garden. You could get inspiration from real life here, or draw from imagination. Are there insects? Birds?

12

Draw your favourite holiday destination on this postcard.
You could write a note to yourself, perhaps describing
how that place makes you feel.

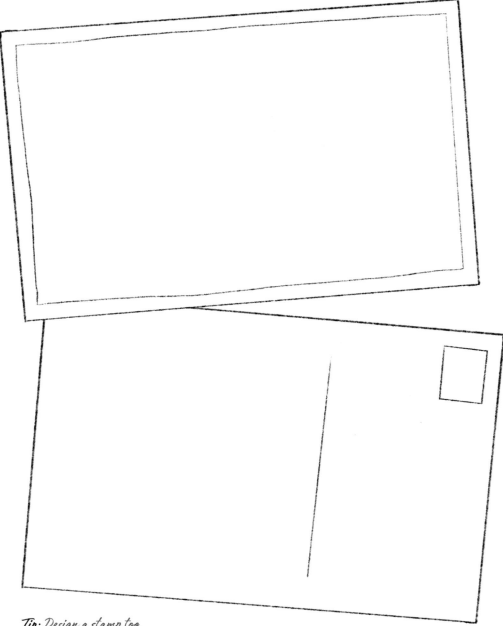

Tip: Design a stamp too.

13

Fill the page with loose drawings of flying birds. Concentrate on their movement and the shapes they make in the sky, rather than worrying about accurately capturing any details.

Tip: Try to convey the energy of the birds.

14 ———————— Fill the page with a mosaic of calming blues, using a variety of art materials.

16 ———————— Sketch your favourite memory.

17

Colours can be described as *clean* (bright and fresh) or *dirty* (hues that are a bit murky). Add swatches of clean and dirty colours below. Enjoy looking out for them when you are out and about or looking at art. Consider which colours you like using more, or perhaps a combination of both? Artists often use a balance of both in their palettes.

Clean

Dirty

Tip: If using paint, the colours straight out of the pan or tube are often clean, whereas dirty colours are often made when you mix colours.

18 ——————— Make a grid of bold, graphic images. You could use any material, perhaps cut paper or pens, to create your shapes. You may want to pick a theme for your design, such as things you love, or nature.

19

Explore using a pen or brush to create sweeping, curving shapes. Relax your wrist and fill the page with loops.

20 ——— Draw a piece of architecture that inspires you.

The Eames House,
Los Angeles, United States.

21 ——————— Fill the page with lots of different colours, allowing the paints to run, overlap, or smudge into each other.

22 ——— Write down how you are feeling. Perhaps explore how your creative journey is going so far. Have you surprised yourself? Is there anything you'd like to do more of?

Journal

23

It's sometimes useful to draw *thumbnails* before starting a large painting or a more sustained piece of art. It's helpful to test compositions and colour palettes, and this preparation helps you feel more confident about starting a bigger piece. Use the space on the opposite page to create some thumbnail sketches for larger pieces of art. You could explore composition options for one piece or many.

Tip: Don't worry about detail or getting things wrong — just get as many little drawings down as possible. Consider which colours you might like to use, or how you could lay things out on the page, but mostly just have fun!

How do you feel about these thumbnails you have created?
Do any inspire you to create a larger piece? If so, go for it!

24 ———— Look through a newspaper or magazine. Find and cut out patterns, textures and colours that you love. Create a piece of art using the cut-out pieces here. Perhaps make an abstract collage, or a scene.

25 ———— Add plants, growing from these roots.

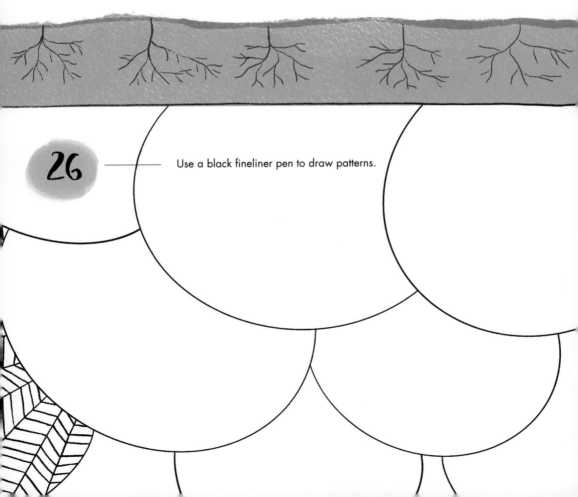

26 ———— Use a black fineliner pen to draw patterns.

27 ——————— Fill the page with lines of calming colours. Enjoy the smooth, steady movement of your pen across the page.

28 ——————— Put on your favourite playlist and create a piece of art inspired by how the music makes you feel. It can be realistic or abstract – see where your thoughts take you.

29 ———— Draw where this path could be, and what could be on it.

30 ———— Add colour or pattern to the sun rays.

31

Choose an object that for some reason makes you feel good. Draw it here. Perhaps it was a gift, or something that used to belong to someone important. Maybe you found the object yourself and have a lovely memory associated with it.

Tip: Perhaps create an abstract background around it.

32

Record your mood using colour. Consider how you feel
and fill the space with colours that help describe your mood.
Record your mood throughout the day.

Optimistic, relaxed

*Tip: You might like to represent your
mood using abstract shapes, mark-
making or even an image.*

33

Draw an object in your house. Keep your marks loose and relaxed, perhaps using blobs of colour to suggest form, then adding a little extra detail on top. You could add tone – using darker colours where you see the shadows.

34

Start drawing a scene or abstract piece on these pages. Then, whenever you see a friend or family member, ask them if they'd like to contribute to the artwork, so that you end up with a piece created by loved ones.

Tip: Remember, there is no wrong way to complete the activity.

Add colour or pattern to the shapes.

36 ——————— Draw the hand of someone special to you. Add as much detail as possible.

Tip: If you aren't able to meet in person, ask your loved one to send you a photo of their hand.

37 ———— Draw your dream house.

38

Complete the design in
any way that you like.

39 ——————— Add faces. Consider expression, hairstyle and character.

40 ———— Draw the scene you see in front of you using only your three favourite colours. Concentrate on the shapes you see, rather than the tones or actual colours.

41 ———— Draw what could be on the horizon.

42 —————— Create colour palettes of things that you see in your day. Look out for colour combinations that help to describe what you see. Perhaps they will be useful in a future drawing.

Tip: *Look for dirty colours as well as clean colours.*

Ice cream van

Clean

Dirty

Could make a great palette for a beach-themed pattern.

43 ————— Create some abstract, imaginary faces using geometric shapes as your starting point.

44 ————— Capture the sky today. You could create a drawing, or take a photo.

45 ——— Relax and spend some time carefully adding patterns to these shapes.

Tip: Sometimes, when doing a very relaxing task, your mind will wander and you will have creative ideas for new projects or pieces of art. Be sure to run with these ideas, and start them, or note them down, as soon as you have the idea.

46 ———— Create some loose, gestural drawings by working quickly. Draw some objects using just a few marks and lines, and don't worry about making mistakes.

47 ——————— Fill the page with as many leaf shapes as you can think of.

48

Feeling confident is an important step towards feeling good about your art, but sometimes it doesn't come easily! Fill this page with positive sentences, mantras or words about your art and creativity. You can always refer back to this page when you need a reminder.

1. I have started a creative journey in this book!

2. I *am* a creative person

Tip: This might take you out of your comfort zone, but try it!

49 ———————— Design a pattern that you'd like on a fabric. Does the design feature repeated motifs? Or perhaps it is completely abstract?

Fill these boxes with colour. Choose colours that create a certain feeling when used together. Or just choose combinations that you really like.

51 ———— Create an image or pattern using the grid.

52 ————

Draw the landmarks in the village, town or city where you live, or in a city that you like.

Tip: You could draw on location, by using your imagination, or from pictures. The drawings can be as detailed as you like.

Tower Bridge, London, England.

53 ———— Draw a piece of furniture in your home, or a piece that you've noticed when out and about.

54 ——————— Create colour swatches of your favourite art materials here. You may like to label them so you can refer back to them.

Tombow ABT
dual brush pens.

55 ———— Fill the page with shells. Perhaps add patterns using mark-making.

56 — Create a different picture on each coloured square.
You may like to use cut paper.

57 ———— Draw your favourite ingredients here.

58 ———— Add colour.

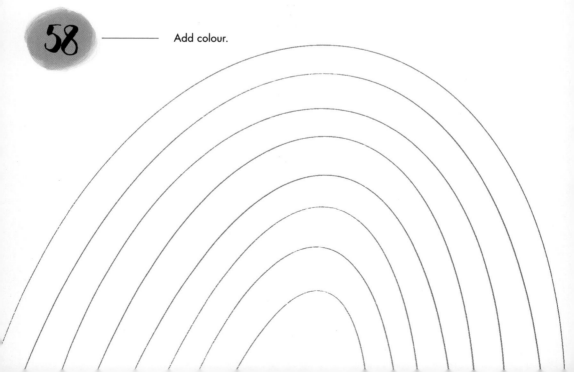

59 ——————— Design a teapot. Consider the shape, materials and colours.

60

Fill the space with colours that get lighter as you go down the page.
You may like to use paints and gradually let the pigment get weaker as
you go down, or if using colouring pencils, apply less pressure as you go.

61 ——— Choose an object that you enjoy the shape of and draw as many variations as you can think of in this space. It could be boats, faces, vases, flowers ...

Add birds to the bird feeder. Perhaps some are perched, and others are flying in. You could draw the garden too.

Write down anything that comes to mind today. You may feel the need to continue writing your thoughts outside of the book, and if so, go for it!

64 ——————— Spend time getting arty with friends, and encouraging others to get their creative juices flowing! Draw someone you know from life, either in person or over a video call. You could take turns drawing each other on each page, while you chat, or draw each other at the same time!

Fill the glass bottles with dried flowers.

66 ———————— Fill the page with greens. Use any material you like to explore texture and mark-making.

67

Spend some time drawing from observation. Maybe focus on just drawing the outlines of what you see.

Tip: Don't worry if your drawings are 'imperfect' – that's OK! Slightly wonky drawing adds character to your work, so be confident and bold.

68 ———————— Create a sunset out of paper. Use cut strips of coloured paper and glue to create your image.

Tip: If you don't have coloured paper, paint some plain paper using the colours you'd like, then wait for it to dry before cutting it.

Create a drawing of an object using your
non-dominant hand. You might like to use
colour, or just focus on the outlines in
one colour. Enjoy the freedom this gives
you to be expressive with your mark-making.

71 ———— Draw something that makes you think of your favourite part of the day.

Tip: Drawing helps us to remember moments in time, and be more present too.

72 ———— Draw art in the gallery frames.

73 ———— Create a design using diamond shapes.
Perhaps add tone to each shape, or colour
from light to dark diagonally across the page.

74 ——————— Quickly note down things that make you happy.

Tip: You may like to return to this page when you are looking for artistic inspiration.

75 ——————— Fill this area with blocks of colour.
You could use pastels, so you create
each block with a single stroke.

76

Turn the coloured blobs into flowers –
perhaps they are growing, or in a bunch,
or maybe you add a pot.

Create a still-life drawing of a few objects. There is no need to worry about making mistakes. You might change your mind about which colours you like, or parts of the drawing might overlap, and that's no problem at all. Just enjoy being creative and exploring what you see in front of you.

Tip: You could use paint or coloured paper to get big areas of colour onto your blank page quickly. This makes the blank space less scary!

Draw your best friend's smile. Or, if you feel like it, their whole face!

79 ———— Use your imagination to turn these coloured blobs into anything you like.

Expand

Create a space where you gather together bits and pieces that inspire you to be creative, or that make you happy. You could start off in a small A5 notebook, and gather any materials, patterns, magazine cuttings or even bits of typography that catch your eye. You could add photos, swatches of colours that you like, even pressed flowers and leaves.

This will become your personal inspiration and ideas book, and you can look through it whenever you need some creative motivation. It may take many years to fill a book completely, but there's no rush.

Tip: If you don't have a blank book to start in, you could stick your gathered materials into an old book, or even keep them loose in a folder.

81 ——————— Design a piece of jewellery.
Who might wear it?

82

Enjoy adding swoops
of green to
this page.

83 ———————— Design some cushions.

84 ———————— Draw the sea.

85 ———— Create a pattern using the grid.

Continue the design.

87 ———— Create a drawing of your favourite meal.
Perhaps use cut paper to create graphic shapes.

88 ———— Take some time to draw vases of flowers in any style you like.

89 —————— Cover the page with interesting shapes. Artist Henri Matisse sometimes filled a space with joyful, abstract, colourful shapes. He often used cut paper, but you could use any material you like.

90 —————— Explore colour blending. Using coloured pencils, add a colour to each circle so that your colours blend where they overlap. Perhaps add more circles – and create more blended colours.

Tip: One way to blend the colours is to press softly and build the colours gradually. If you are using watercolour pencils, try blending with a little bit of water and a clean brush.

91 ———— Design some candlestick holders. They could be simple or ornate.

92 ———— Choose a word that describes how you feel when you are being creative. Use expressive lettering to draw the word below.

93 ———————— Create a drawing of an object without looking at the page. Look only at the object you can see, except when you change colour.

Tip: You will probably end up with a drawing that looks a bit messy, but that's great! Enjoy the time feeling free to be expressive and making bold marks.

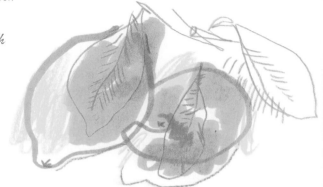

94 ———— Create a diary of your day using images. Draw something in each box to represent something that has happened or might happen.

95 ———————

Fill the page with imaginary succulents.
Enjoy designing pots for them too.

96

Design a mobile. Perhaps
simple shapes are hanging,
or more complex objects.

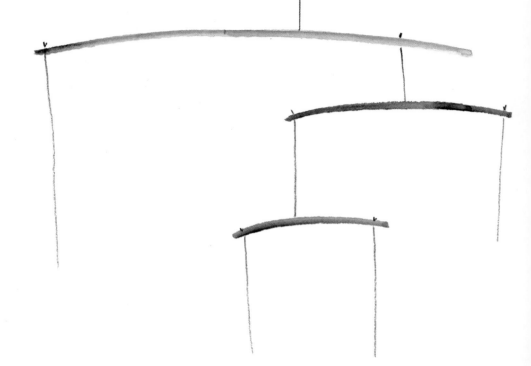

97

Look up at the sky on a cloudy day. What shapes and objects can you see in the clouds? Draw them here.

98 ———————— Design your own paper stationery, including a logo for your name. Sketch some ideas for motifs of logos you could add to letters, or to the footer of your emails.

99

Create a city skyline. Consider how varying colours and tones can give your images different moods.

Create a colouring sheet for yourself or friends and family. Draw ideas here, or continue adding to this image. You could draw the colouring sheet on a separate piece of paper, and then create copies using a photocopier.

Expand

101 ———— Fill the space with abstract shapes to make a design or pattern.

102 ———— Draw the contents of the jars.

103 ———— Continue the design and then add colour or pattern.

104

Choose a piece of fruit and draw it using three different materials. Notice which materials you enjoy the most. Are there certain qualities you like in each of your drawings?

Tip: When life gives you lemons, draw them!

Use this space to write your journal. Consider how you can allow yourself to truly express your creativity, and be playful with your art.

106

Walk around your home, or look around a café if you are out and about. Without thinking about it too much, draw objects or little scenes that stand out to you. These could be line drawings, or you may like to add colour and tone. Perhaps layer the drawings over each other.

Tip: This will help you form a memory of this moment in time, and is a record of the things that caught your eye.

107

Add details to these coloured blobs so they become trees or plants.

Design a colourful pair of curtains.

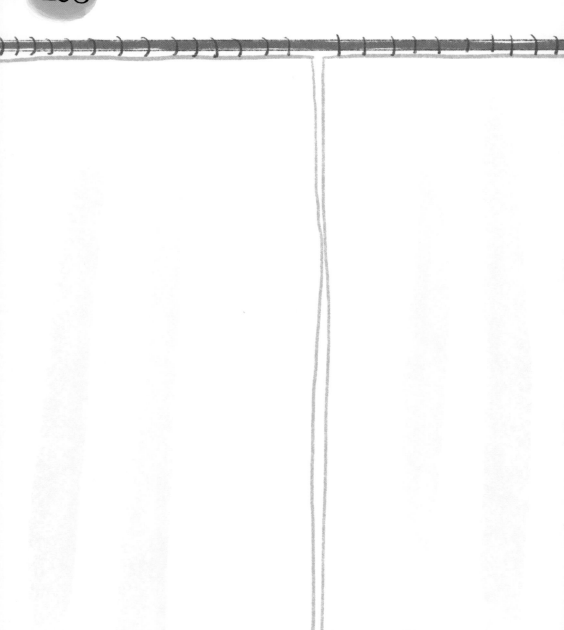

109 ———————— Continue adding small geometric shapes to fill the space.

110 ———————— Blend coloured pencils in the boxes. *Tip: Colouring in the same direction will encourage calm.*

111 ———————— Design patterns using warm colours.

112 ———————— Fill the page with coloured polka dots.

113 ———— Look back at the encouraging statements you wrote in activity 48. Choose one which makes you feel empowered and write it here, using creative typography.

114 —————— Do a wild scribble. Could it become something else?

115 —————— Fill with blue droplets.

116

Draw a bunch of flowers and enjoy making marks to show the petals and leaves. Have fun with the shapes and don't worry too much about the end result – just let your mind relax as you draw.

117 ———— Design some stamps.

118 ———— Draw your favourite thing to do.

119 ————————— Use this space to express how you feel at this moment in time, using art. How can the colours you use, or the marks you make, help to describe your emotions?

Fill the circles with patterns and colour. Be as expressive as you like.

121 ——————— Explore using cut paper only to create faces. Sometimes drawing with pens can feel like a bit too much pressure to be precise, but drawing with scissors can help you to relax because it doesn't have to be accurate at all.

Tip: You could layer different shapes and colours to create the faces.

Draw what you might see under the waves.

123 ———— Think about how you can bring more colour to your art by adding bright backgrounds. While drawing from life, try putting colours behind what you see.

124

——————

Draw an object, but take up this entire page.
Be bold and use energetic marks.

125 ——————— Draw your favourite outfit. You could use cut paper to create the shapes.

126

Choose a subject – perhaps an object you like the shape of, or the corner of a room – and draw what you see without looking at the page *or* lifting your pencil off the page.

Tip: Continuous line drawings are tricky but enjoy letting your eyes wander over what you see, and feel the peaceful movement of the pencil on the paper. Don't worry if the end result looks a bit chaotic!

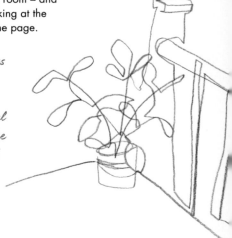

127

We can learn by making mistakes, even if they are intentional! Draw a scene, object or face twice below. First, draw it with something deliberately in the wrong place. Then draw it again but with all the elements in the correct place.

Draw a still life or scene without worrying at all about accuracy. You could have objects overlapping each other, use colours that are different from what you see, or more exaggerated, and even add in imaginary elements. Go with the flow and how you feel in the moment.

*Newlyn,
Cornwall, England.*

Tip: Remember, there is no such thing as 'bad' art! Just enjoy the process of creating and using the materials. If you start thinking you aren't doing a good job — remind yourself that you're having fun and that's all that matters!

129 ——————— Enjoy practising drawing. Find an image that you like in a book. It could be a photograph, or a piece of art. Turn the image upside down, and then draw it here. Once you have finished, turn this book around to see what you have drawn.

Tip: Drawing upside down is a great way to improve accuracy in our drawing, because it encourages us to look carefully at the actual shapes we can see, rather than drawing what we think we see. Accuracy isn't always important, but if you'd like to improve, practising is the best thing to do!

130 ———

Draw a piece of fruit
using both hands at once.
Hold a pencil in each hand,
and move them at the same
time to 'sculpt' your shape.

131 ———— Choose one of your favourite pieces of art and do your own version here. Perhaps you create it in different materials, or use the same subject but draw it in your own way. Add your own personality to the drawing.

132

Draw something that moves. It can be tricky to draw something that is not staying still, but see the funny side of it! Put your marks down very quickly, and enjoy making lots of fast, incomplete studies, rather than a 'final' image.

Tip: You may find that you like the energy of the quick drawings, and that they describe your subject quite well!

133 ———— Fill the space with strawberries. Use strokes of red to create the shapes. Have fun with the forms!

134 ———— Create a colour palette below using swatches of colour that make you feel energised.

135　——————

Choose somewhere comfortable to sit, where you can use the book and also feel relaxed, such as a comfy sofa or even in bed. Draw what you see in front of you.

Tip: Be expressive, and let your pencil glide over the page with confidence.

136 ———— Continue the wavy lines in any material you like.

137 ——————— Create different textures in the boxes.
You could use a variety of colours and materials.

138 ——————— Continue adding green squares to the space.
Use any materials you like.

139

Enjoy studying an object as a whole and also close up, to really get to know it. Choose anything – perhaps a tree, a building or a person. Draw the whole thing, and then focus on the smaller elements you can see.

Tip: You may want to make some quick sketches of your chosen subject to get a feel for it. Or just go for it. There's no wrong way to approach this activity.

140

Draw some buildings on location. Drawing something as complex as this may seem daunting, so simplify the buildings as much as you can. Identify the key shapes first, before adding in the details.

London, England.

141 ———— Write down the names of all the people who are special to you. Perhaps explore using calligraphy and cursive writing.

142 ———— Add swatches of all the colours you like, using any materials you have.

143

Use your favourite materials to draw an object of your choice. Perhaps something you see every day. Try mixing materials and exploring how they interact.

144

———

Think about the moods you are feeling today.
What colours or shapes represent your feelings?

145

———

Add texture and pattern to the leaf shapes.

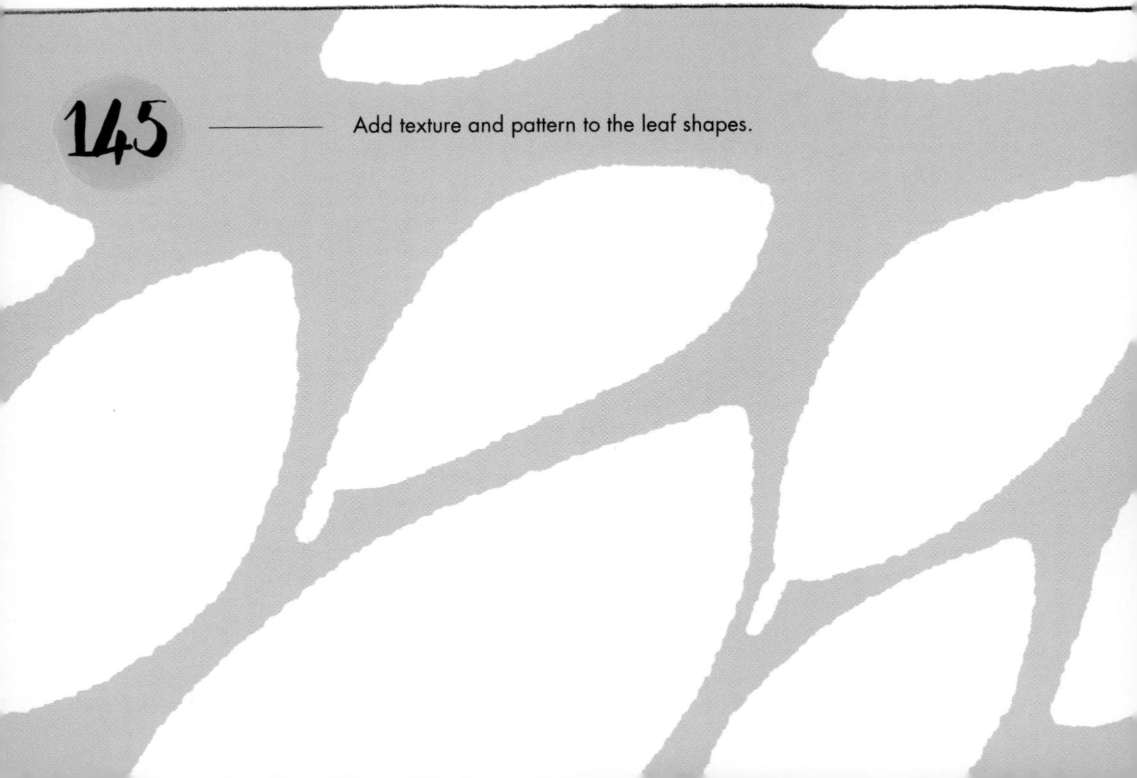

146 ——————— Draw a scene using only cut-out paper shapes.
Don't worry about accuracy, just enjoy thinking about how you
could portray what you see using shapes and colour.

148 ———— Draw something that makes you feel good.

149 ———— Create a design on each tile.

Take some time to write freely.
Perhaps describe how art, or
being creative, makes you feel.

Journal

151 ———— Continue adding coloured lines.

152 ———— Design a pattern using soft shapes and marks.

153

Draw an object using both hands at once. Use a different material in each hand and use them at the same time to create your drawing. It may feel a bit messy and difficult but it's a great way to feel freer with your drawing and helps you learn to be less precious about your marks.

154 ——————— Use this page to really enjoy abstract colour, in any way you like.

Continue the drawing and then add colour.

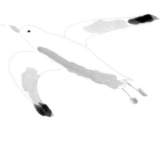

156 ———— Draw an animal or person using a variety of materials. Notice how the different materials give different qualities to your art.

157 ——————— It can be useful to learn more about yourself. Think about all the things that make you happy – who? What? Where? Write about or draw one of them here.

158 ——————— Draw how you feel today. Perhaps use abstract shapes.

———————— Fill with hearts.

160 —————— Relax as you continue adding warm colours to this page. You may like to continue with the curves, or try something completely different.

161

Explore using different colours next to each other to find colour combinations you like. Draw a circle of colour, and then try different colours around it.

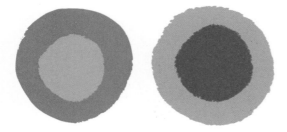

162 ——— Start a sketchbook to keep a record of locations that make you feel great.

Expand

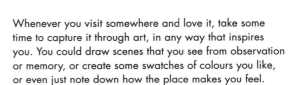

The Highlands, Scotland.

Whenever you visit somewhere and love it, take some time to capture it through art, in any way that inspires you. You could draw scenes that you see from observation or memory, or create some swatches of colours you like, or even just note down how the place makes you feel.

It could be useful to keep paper or a small sketchbook, and some art materials with you whenever you take a trip to somewhere new, or you may choose to make your art when you return home and have all your materials around you. Either is great, but drawing on location will give you the most memorable experience.

You could use a scrapbook, sketchpad, notebook or even a collection of loose paper kept in a folder.

Perhaps use bright colours to help express happiness, and remember that the drawings can be very quick and spontaneous.

Tip: Allow yourself to feel the joy as you paint and draw! When you create a piece of art based on a location, it helps us remember it better in the future, and is a record of how we felt at the time.

163

Draw the moon. You could add stars to the background using white pastel or pencil.

164

Look at an object, such as a flower or something you treasure, for five minutes. Trace the outline with your eyes, and notice the shapes and angles carefully. Then put the object somewhere you can't see it, and draw it from memory.

165 ——————— Draw a beach.

166 ——————

When drawing part of a scene, there's no pressure to fill the page to the edge. Draw something you love, from life or from a photo, and focus on just capturing the elements you really love to observe. You could leave the edges of your drawing loose and 'unfinished' to give your art energy.

*Mousehole,
Cornwall, England.*

167 ———— Turn these coloured marks into a garden.

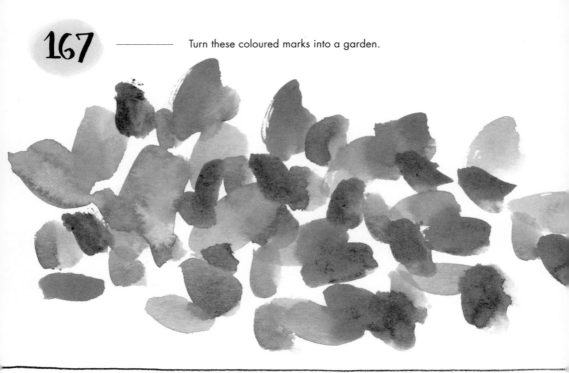

168 ———— Draw your own mouth, smiling.

169

Create an image by colouring in
the circles. You may like to create
a scene, or abstract pattern.

A blank page can feel daunting, but there is a simple way to feel more confident about starting a drawing. Loosely and boldly add a big block of colour to the blank page opposite using paint or coloured paper. Once you've made a big mark, you've already conquered the blank page and can draw on top of it with confidence! Once it has dried, draw a landscape or skyline on top of your background.

Here, I painted a blue background using acrylic paint.

I decided that the blue could represent the sky, and used watercolour, pastel and coloured pencils to draw a skyline on top and beneath the background.

Tip: If you are drawing while out and about, you can prepare sketchbook pages beforehand by adding blocks of colours to the pages. When you come to use them, just choose whichever background feels right at the time.

One World Trade Center, New York, United States.

Continue drawing lines and then add colour to the sections.

173 ———— Write out your name, using thick shapes to make the letters.
Then fill the letters with decoration, or objects that represent you.

174 ———— Fill this area with coloured rings.

Draw fruit using simple shapes to create a pattern.

Create a space in your home where you feel comfortable being creative.

Expand

Make yourself a feel-good art play area!

Your creative space doesn't have to be a large space, and could be more of a 'kit' in a drawer or pencil case that you can access easily and take to a table or cosy chair.

Fill your chosen space, or kit, with art materials that you love to use, along with any inspiration you have gathered.

The idea is to make creating art as easy for yourself as possible – so if your materials are easy to grab, and you already know the space where you can create comfortably, then you've already removed some very big hurdles!

Consider what mood or atmosphere you prefer to create art in, and think about how you can cultivate this.
Is there a music playlist you could make to assist you?
Or a radio station?

Tip: Personally, I find that it helps to see all my art materials, as it inspires me to pick them up and be creative for a few minutes. So I like to keep them all out on a table. I also prefer to have my chores and piles of to-do lists tidied away before I start!

177 ———————— Doodle!

178 ———————— Create a colour palette below using swatches
of colour that make you feel peaceful and relaxed.

179 ———— Draw the sky today.

180 ———— Colour the scarves, then design your own.

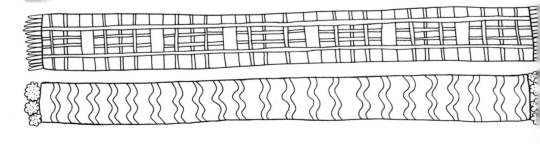

Keep adding straight lines to this design, working
from the outside in. Then add colour to the shapes.

182 ———·——— Continue to fill
the space, then
add tone.

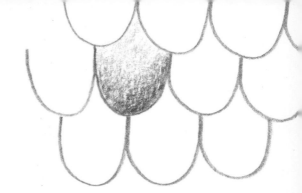

183 ——————

Draw the rest of this harbour scene. Add the sea, boats, and perhaps more of the pier.

184

————

Make some drawings using blocks of colour to create your forms. You could use bits of paper to create the main shapes you see.

The Golden Palace, Kyoto, Japan.

Tip: Maybe use online maps to take a virtual holiday to a location that you'd love to visit.

185 ———— Create a design or pattern using the grid.

186 ———— Sometimes, you may feel frustrated about your own art, so it can help to focus on what you like in other people's art. Write or draw what you like about the work of other artists.

187 ———— Design a toy town. Don't worry about perspective. Be playful!

188 ——————— Draw what you can see out of your window.

189

We can't always visit our favourite places, but we can look at them!
Use online maps to visit a location that makes you feel happy.
Have a look around and draw what you see.

The Maldives.

Tip: You could set yourself a time limit to draw, or perhaps challenge yourself to draw five images of your virtual trip!

190 ——————— Draw the highlight of your week so far.

191 ——————— Fill with flowers.

192

Write whatever is on your mind. Let your thoughts flow freely, and use more paper if needed. Have you felt inspired by anything this week?

193

Make a
mess with
pastels!

194 ———— Create a colour palette below using swatches of colour that make you feel joyful.

195 ———— Draw lots of clouds, adding texture and colour.

196 ——————— Draw lots of colourful circles, all different sizes, to create a happy pattern.

197 ———— Draw the rest of this river. See where your marks and lines take you.

198 ———— Draw a bird. It could be imaginary.

199 ——— Practise using your feelings to lead your art. Find something you'd like to draw – a view that you like, or part of your home that you love. Paint or draw the scene while channelling how you feel right now.

Tip: Consider how the marks and colours you use can express your mood.

Humlebæk, Denmark.

Here, I felt very relaxed looking at the sea and trees, which seemed to almost roll into each other. I used the same green in the foliage and the sea, to emphasise their connection. I decided to use broad brush strokes, and worked slowly to capture the feeling of calm.

200 ———————— Artist Faith Ringgold paints her stories onto fabric quilts. Design a quilt that tells your own personal story about something that brings you joy. It could be a memory, objects that you love, or an imaginary situation. You could add in elements of pattern too, and add a border to your scene by adding block colours to the outside of the quilt.

201

Enjoy exploring one material.
What different marks can you make?

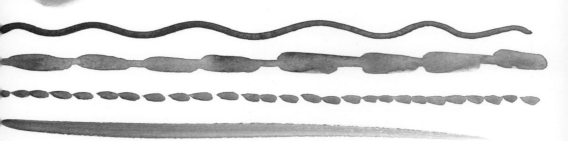

202

Using these coloured blobs as starting points, create lots of flowers. They don't need to be at all realistic – explore how abstract you can go.

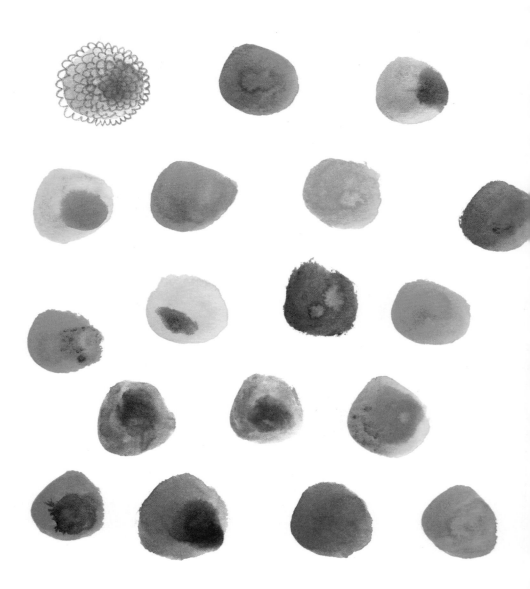

Continue the scene. What else could be
on this table, in front of the sea?

204 ———— Continue adding circles.

205 ———— Add colour and pattern to the bird.

206 ——————— Draw someone who is important to you.

207 —————— Paint abstract colours and textures onto separate pieces of loose paper. You could use a mixture of different materials. Allow everything to dry, then cut the paper into shapes and create a piece of art below.

Tip: You may like to explore different compositions before you decide to stick any of your shapes down.

208 ———— Add plants and flowers to the pots.

 209 ———— Draw or write a memory that makes you happy.

Make marks or designs based on the circular form.

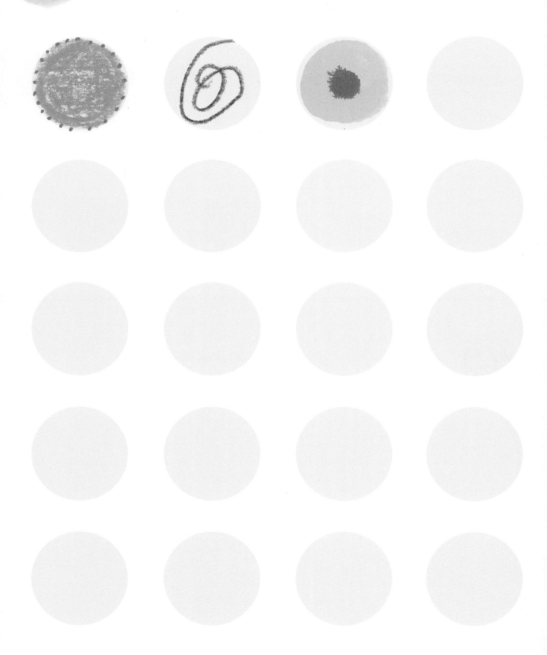

211 —————— Create some mini compositions. These could be ideas for future paintings – perhaps abstracts or little scenes.

Tip: You don't need to add much detail – just block out the key shapes with colour.

212 —————— Draw four plants that you like. You could just draw outlines, or perhaps add colour and tone too, depending on how you feel.

213 ——————— Create a diary of your day using images rather than words. Draw something in each box to represent part of your day.

214 ———————— Fill the page with doodles.
Relax and draw whatever you feel.

215 ————— Draw some of your materials,
using the material itself.

Create a mood calendar using colour to express how you feel on each day. There's no right or wrong colour to use – just go with whatever colour feels best. Perhaps add more than one colour each day.

Monday	
Tuesday	
Wednesday	
Thursday	
Friday	
Saturday	
Sunday	
Monday	
Tuesday	
Wednesday	
Thursday	
Friday	
Saturday	
Sunday	

217 ———————— Add colour to this page, and allow
the materials to blend into each other.

218

Draw a map of your country. You could add your favourite places, or colour in areas that you would like to visit.

219 —— Explore smudging warm colours together.

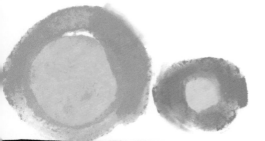

220 —— Design pairs of cosy socks.

221

————————

Draw a corner of your home that you love.
Perhaps exaggerate the colours so it looks very vivid.

222 —————— Design patterns using cool colours.

Tip: To keep the edges of your patterns straight, you could stick masking tape along the edge of the pattern before you start, and then carefully peel it off once you've finished.

Draw shapes and then add tone.

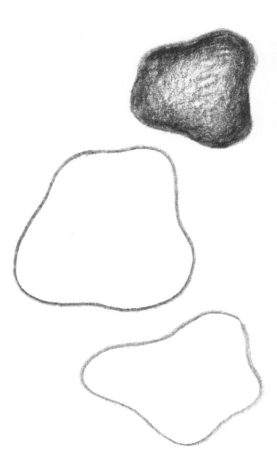

224

Fill the page with lines of energetic colours. Perhaps the shape of your lines could help convey energy too.

225 ———— Draw something from your week that made you happy. You might draw this from memory or by observing it.

226 ———— Add a fire to the fireplace.

227 —————— Fill the page with drawings
of foliage and flowers.

228

Draw a self-portrait on a day that you feel great.
You could use a mirror, or work from a photograph.

Tip: It might be easiest to hold a smile if you keep your mouth closed ... plus, drawing teeth can be quite tricky!

229 ——————— Draw somewhere you love, multiple times. Perhaps draw it when you are in different moods, or in a variety of weathers or seasons. See if you notice different things about the view each time, or if your drawings reflect your mood. You may like to add notes to your drawings about how you were feeling.

Tip: You could choose somewhere local to where you live, or somewhere you frequently visit.

230 ———— Design a pattern using simple, geometric shapes.

231 ———— Draw a dog.

232 ———————— Fill this space with squares.

233 ———— Make drawings from observation in the boxes.
They can be any scene you see – indoors or outdoors.

Tip: The more you practise drawing from
observation, the more confident you will become.

236 ———————— Using any materials you like, create a
representation of the feeling of love.

237 ———————— Design a personal flag. What symbols and colours could you use to
represent yourself?

238 ———— Continue adding blues and greens to this page to create a tranquil piece of art.

239

Describe your ideal creative space. Understanding what we need in order to feel relaxed is a useful step. Perhaps you enjoy music and background noise, or like to be in a quiet space. Maybe it needs to be tidy around you, or you prefer it messy!

240

Create a 'feel-good' landscape on the opposite page. Look at a photo of some scenery, or draw from life. Pick out the joyful colours you can see and exaggerate them. You could use this space below to add some swatches of colours you find joyous before you begin.

Near Crieff,
Perthshire, Scotland.

241 ——————— Use this space to explore your materials. Keep building up your image with lines and shapes until you create something that makes you feel happy. You could use cut paper to create big, coloured shapes.

242 — Use light-coloured pencils or pastels to fill the space with stars.

243 — Continue the pattern.

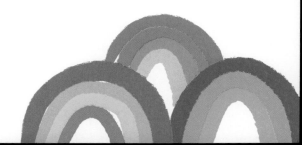

244 ———— Add colour.

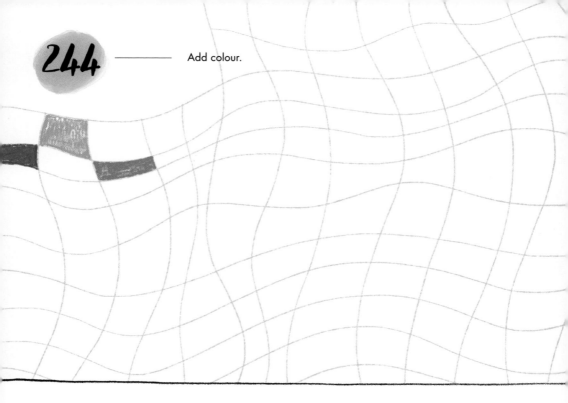

245 ———— Visit a museum and draw your favourite exhibit there.

246 ———— Draw your own hand. Follow the outline of your wrist, hand and fingers with your eye, and as you do so, slowly draw what you see. Look carefully at the distances and shapes between your fingers, and take your time.

Draw concentric rings of colours to fill the space.

248 ———————

Some zoos and wildlife parks have camera footage that you can watch online. Have a look to see what you can find, and draw some animals from the footage.

249 —————— Draw lines in a range of materials, and then use different materials on top to see how they interact.

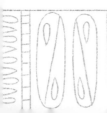 **250** —————— Continue the patterns. You could also add colour.

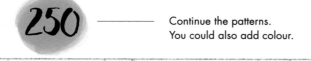

251

———— Hold your pencil at the very end and make a drawing of something you can see.

Tip: Your picture is likely to look a little bit messy but that's great! The aim of this activity is to help you get used to losing control while drawing, and to see that it's fun to create, regardless of the outcome.

252 ——— Draw a sky in each strip. Consider the different colours and textures you might find.

253

Draw a sleeping pet, or person. Take your time and enjoy observing them feeling relaxed.

254 —————— Design the cover of a travel book,
depicting somewhere that you'd love to go.

255 ——————— Add happy faces to the suns.

Design a plant pot.

257 ———— Look at the colour of the skin on your wrist or back of your hand. Create swatches of the colours that you see, and then mix the colour that matches your skin the closest.

258 ———— Draw or describe a happy memory from this week.

259

Sometimes we need to take our mind off anxious thoughts and worries.
Creating something calming and beautiful can be a good thing
to do in these moments when we need to give our minds a break.
Draw something you find beautiful.

260 ———— Add blue curved lines to this page using any materials you like.

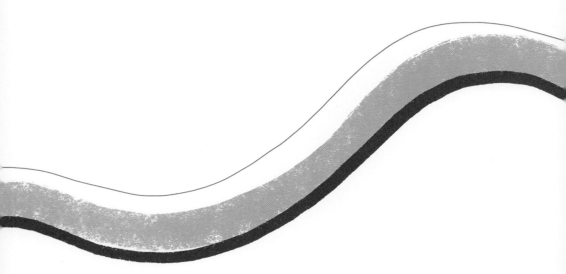

261

The blank page can be daunting, so you can always start by quickly applying colour to your background. Use this background as a starting point for your own piece of art.

262 ——————— Draw a dream.

263 ——————— Look closely at the grain
in a piece of wood and draw it here.

Tip: You could use the side of a
pencil to make the soft, loose lines.

264 ——— Create a forest using loose, quick brush marks to paint your trees. Are there wildflowers growing? Animals? Or is it dense with trees?

265 ———— Use mark-making to express how you feel today. How does the way you use your materials help to convey a feeling?

266 ———— Notice the beauty in the everyday. Find somewhere peaceful and create a pencil sketch of a household object that wouldn't be your usual choice of subject for a piece of art.

Design a blanket or throw.

268

The artist Vincent van Gogh painted skies with brush marks that swirled around. Take a look at *The Starry Night*, and create your own swirling night sky.

Make a drawing at your favourite time of day. Aim to capture the colours and mood that makes that time distinct.

Evening. Perranuthnoe, Cornwall, England.

270

Create a drawing for someone special and then show them. You could choose to depict something you know they like, or create something more abstract.

Tip: Making things for other people is a brilliant way to make yourself feel good at the same time as spreading joy to others.

271 ——— Add life to this
rock pool.

Design the mugs.

Add colour to the shapes.

274 ———— Add colour to this design.

275 ———————— Focus on the positives in your art. What do you love about what you've created so far? What have you enjoyed and what has made you proud? Write down your thoughts.

276   ———————   It can be joyful and surprising to combine the unexpected in your art. Choose an animal and a fruit to create a pattern. It can be silly!

277

Draw a patchwork quilt. The squares could be patterned or plain.

278 ———— Paint a jungle.

279 ———— Fill with smiles.

280 ——————— Draw your eyes.

281 ——————— Continue creating a pattern based on this one that has been started.

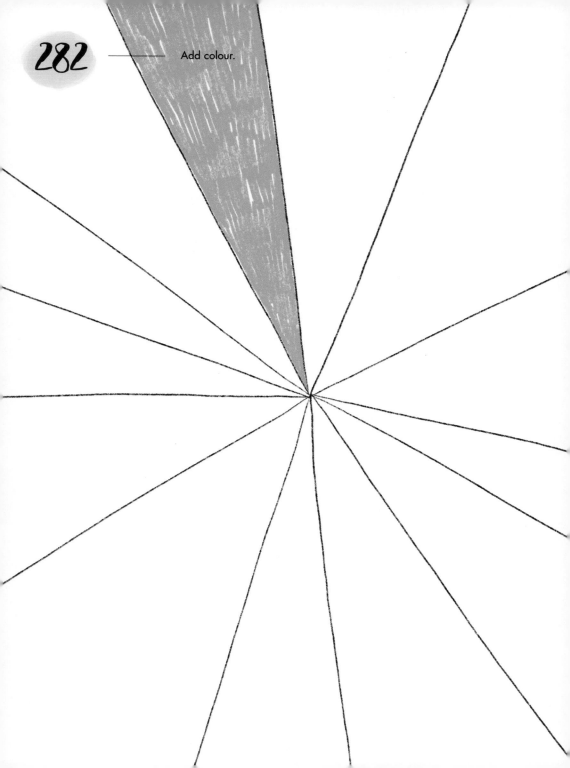

282

Add colour.

283 ——————— Draw butterflies.

284 ——— Write down anything you are feeling today, including anything you are excited about or feel grateful for.

—————— Draw the rest of the cityscape.

286 —————— Note down a story or conversation that made you laugh.
Illustrate a scene or something that reminds you of the funniest part.

287 —————— Draw the weather today.

Design a pot for
these plants.

289

Fill the white areas with patterns that are joyful.
Explore happy colours and shapes.

290

There is no wrong way to approach a drawing, and a good way to start is to be led by your feelings. Look at the sky and consider how it makes you feel. Use these feelings to inform the marks and materials you use.

Thurnham, Lancashire, England.

Tip: Here, I felt like the sun rays were making me feel happy and full of energy, so I drew them quickly using lines of pen.

Add decorations and lights
to the strings.

293 ———————— Buy yourself a bunch of flowers and draw the blooms.

294 ───── We don't need to live near amazing wildlife in order to draw it. There are plenty of free nature live cams online, so we can draw animals in their natural habitat without disturbing them. Look for a live stream and draw what you see.

Tip: Seeing the animals moving around (rather than static in a photo) can help us understand their 3D shape.

Tip: If you see a pose that you love, you can pause the stream and take a bit more time to draw it.

Draw a different landscape in each strip below.

296

We all have barriers that get in the way of us creating art. These might be related to time, materials, worries, and pressure that we put on ourselves. Note down everything that holds you back, then write down how you can actively overcome each barrier.

Barrier:	Action:
Worried about doing art 'wrong'	Remind myself that there is no 'wrong' and challenge myself to make mistakes and be playful when I create. Focus on having fun!

297 —————— Set up a still life using items that you love. It could be a few things or many. Position them in a way that looks visually pleasing to you and draw what you see, using any materials you like. It can be something you take a long time over, or capture very quickly.

Tip: Before you start, look carefully at your still life and think about where the middle is, and where the middle should be in your picture. Be sure to leave enough room on the page to fit everything in.

298 ———— Add colours to this design, considering which hues will go well together.

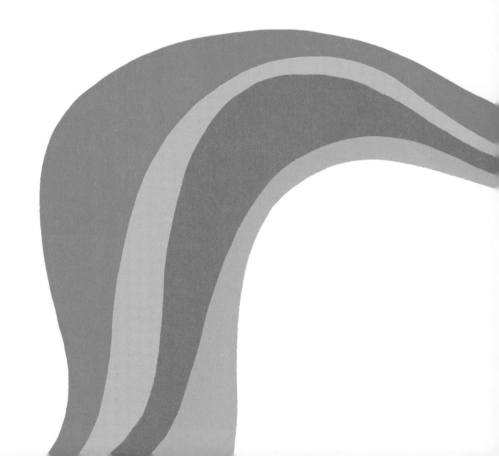

Draw what you might find in and around the greenhouse.

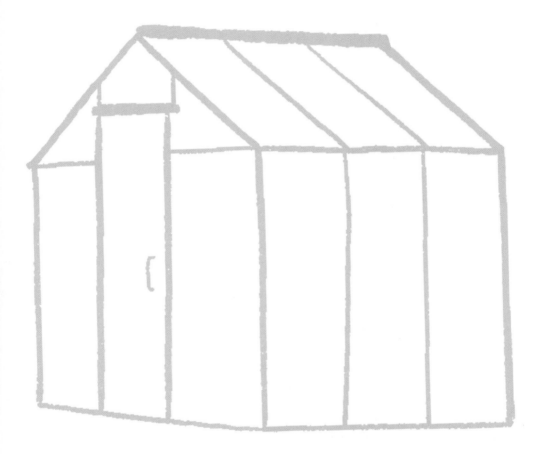

300 ——— Choose a subject that has variations. For example, trees, plants, chairs, or even faces. Draw as many different variations as you can on the opposite page. You could space them evenly so that they form an appealing composition.

Tip: Notice the differences between your subjects. Are they different colours? Shapes? Textures?

Draw the rest of the image.

302 —————— Write a letter to someone special (or to yourself). Let them know what makes them important to you, and what you like about them. You could also add a decorative border.

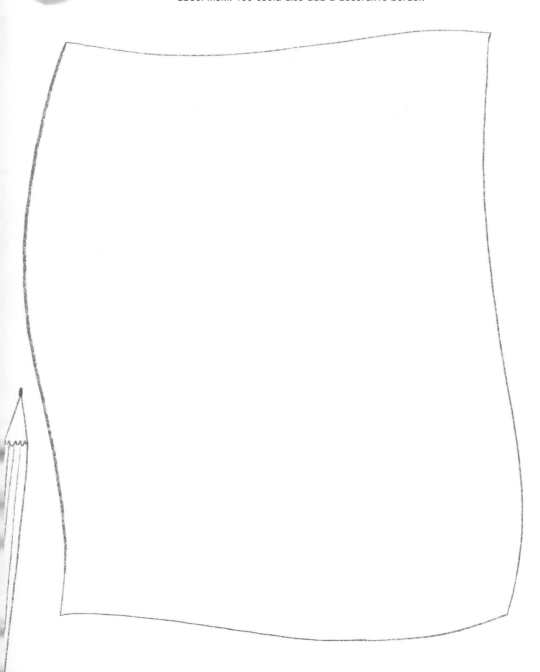

303 —————— Design the base of a lamp. You could design a lampshade too.

304

Add a scene below this sky. Perhaps there is a town on the horizon, or the sky is above a forest or beach.

305 ———— Draw things that remind you of your favourite season.

306 ———— Write a positive word using colour and pattern to create the letters.

Design some vases. Focus on making them as colourful as possible. You could paint bits of paper and then, once dry, cut them up to make different vase shapes.

Tip: You could also collage bits of pattern you have collected from magazines or scrap paper.

Add colour to this abstract scene using a
variety of different materials or patterns.

309 ———— Create a cartoon sketch of your day.

310 ———— Continue the pattern.

311

Visit a park or green space and draw something you see when you are there. Sit on a bench to draw, or make a quick standing sketch. You don't need to show anyone your art if you don't want to, just do it for yourself in whichever way works best for you. One of the hardest steps towards being creative is overcoming the 'I'm not good enough' voice. Well, you are!

Tip: Perhaps pack just a few pencils or other art materials. That way you don't have to take too long deciding what to use, and you make it as easy as possible to get started.

Artist Piet Mondrian created bold, graphic compositions using geometric blocks in a limited colour palette. Take a look at his work, and then add colour to complete your own composition.

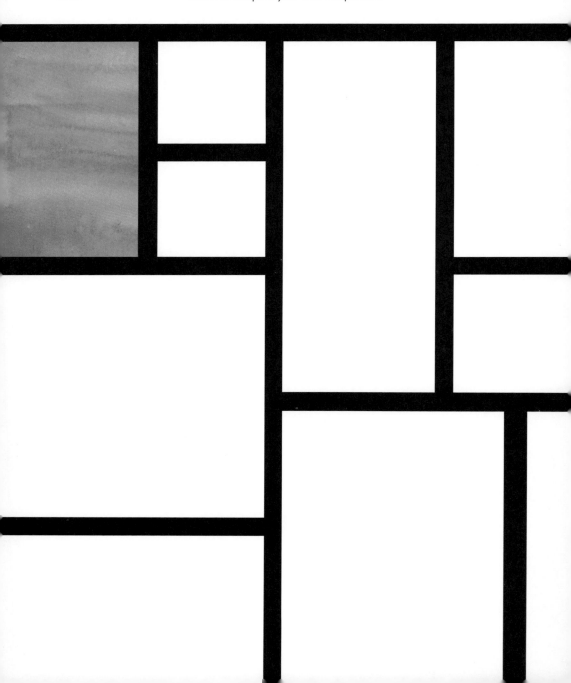

Design your own pieces of pottery.

Add funny animals or characters to these eyes.
The sillier the better. Have a giggle!

315 ———————— Gather some art materials you feel comfortable with and choose a place to sit where you feel peaceful. Take some deep, calming breaths, and then draw what you can see – this could be anything you like, something close up or a whole scene. Do your best to focus on capturing what you see in front of you, bringing your thoughts back to your art whenever you find them drifting.

316

Use deep blues and purples to draw outer space. You could create stars and galaxies using white paint flicks.

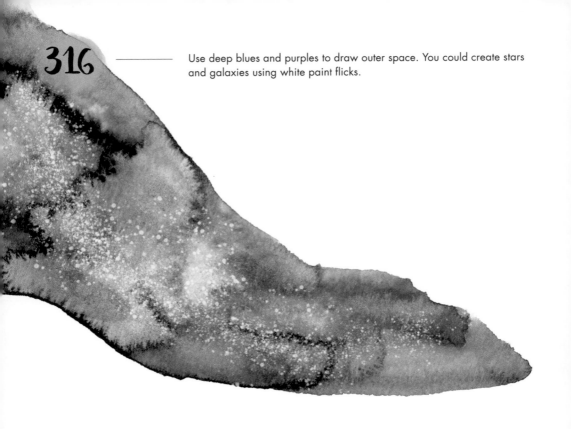

318 ———— Look online for a live stream of a coral reef, and draw what you see. It can be relaxing to watch the colourful fish move about!

Tip: You may have to work quickly to capture the colours and shapes of the fish, so perhaps lay out your materials in front of you so you can grab them as soon as you decide on a colour.

319 —————— Find a photo that you really like. Stick it in here and then design a frame around it.

320 ——— Draw a wildflower meadow. It could be abstract.

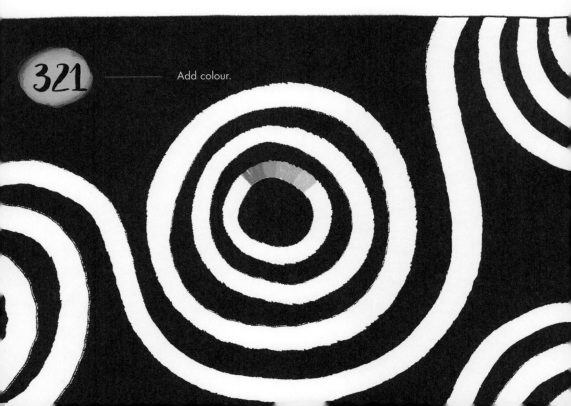

321 ——— Add colour.

322 ———— Take a break. Go somewhere you won't be disturbed and put on some calming music. Draw what comes to mind.

323 ———— Continue painting ferns.

Take some time to write your thoughts today. They don't have to be about anything in particular. See where your writing takes you.

325 ——— Fill the page with swoops of green using a variety of materials.

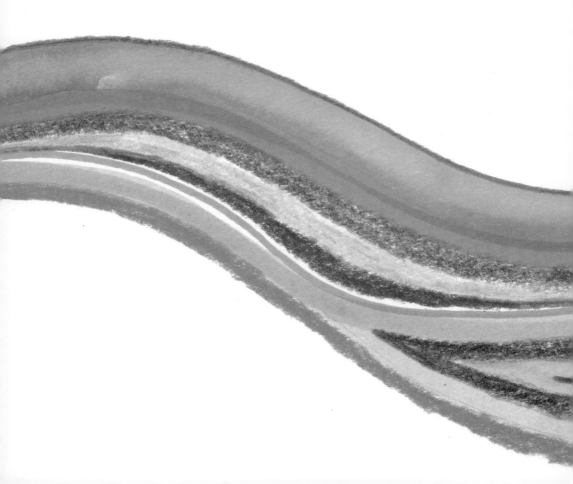

326 ———————— Design a pair of trainers.

327

Look at the world around you but imagine the saturation is turned right up! Exaggerating the colours you see can be a simple way to add more joy into your art. Draw something from life, but emphasise the bright colours you see, or even swap out all the duller colours for different bright ones.

328 ——————— Create an abstract, geometric design
using calming pastel colours.

Tip: Perhaps use coloured pencils and
blend the colours where the shapes cross.

329 ———— When you aren't sure what to draw, a very good place to start is with what makes you happy. If you're not sure what this is, then draw lots of things!

Tip: Find what you love to draw and run with it! It's completely OK to draw the same thing over and over again if that is what makes you happy.

330 ——————— Create an image of water.

331 ——————— Continue drawing straight lines in these triangles to complete the design.

332 ———— Draw a storm while sat in the comfort of the cosy indoors.

333 ———— Draw tropical birds on these perches.

334 ————— Allow yourself to feel all your emotions as you create. Make marks or splodges of colour on this page as you think about how you feel. Go with the flow and let yourself be drawn to certain shapes or colours.

335 —————— Add flowers to the stems. Perhaps add insects and bees too.

336 —————— Add colour and pattern to the spiral.

Use this page to let off steam!

Tip: So that you don't worry about your materials bleeding through the paper, you could tape down an extra piece of paper on top of this one.

338 ——— Draw a plant or bunch of flowers without putting too much emphasis on it being completely accurate. Just relax into the task and enjoy looking at the shapes and colours you see. There's no need to set a time limit for this task.

Tip: Add your marks to the page with confidence!

Tip: Drawing is a great time to process your feelings. So let your mind wander as you paint and draw.

339 —————— Draw an absurd scene and make yourself laugh! Art doesn't need to be serious. What would it look like if something unusual was flying? Or if a vehicle or animal was doing something unexpected?

340 —————— Add your own pattern and colour.

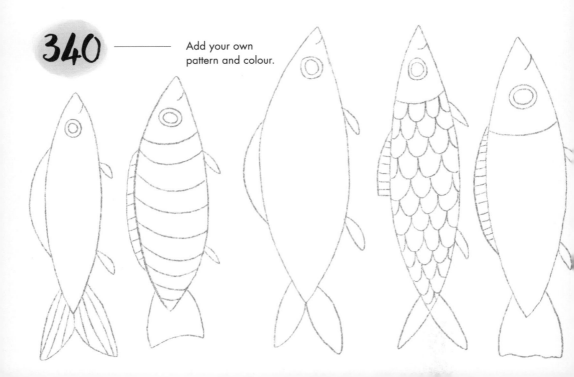

Draw the rest of the flowers.

342 ———— Add colour to the wavy grid to make a pattern.

343 ———————— Draw symbols or images to represent each season.

344 ———————— Look at the colours in your favourite painting. Create swatches of all the different hues you see. Maybe do a sketch of the piece too, and note down what it is that you like about that particular artwork.

Create a design or drawing in each box, inspired by the shape inside.

346 ————— Explore collage, using bits of paper to create a piece of art based on the natural world.

347 ———— Design a t-shirt. Perhaps use the space around it to experiment with ideas, colours and designs.

348 ———— Use pressed flowers and leaves to create art.

Being among nature can be very soothing, as can using it in your art. When the season is right, buy or find some flowers at the side of a path or in your garden. Use scissors to cut just a few – rather than taking more than you need.

Arrange your flowers on a piece of watercolour paper, ready to be pressed. You ideally want to use watercolour paper above and below the flowers, and some extra sheets of plain paper for padding too.

Tip: If you don't have watercolour paper, try other absorbent papers such as kitchen roll or toilet roll.

Pile some heavy books on top of your paper, flowers and leaves. Leave it be for a couple weeks, and then lift up the layers to see what you have created!

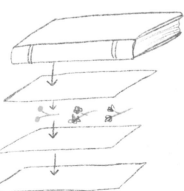

Books

Watercolour paper

Flowers/leaves

Watercolour paper

Paper

You could use your pressed flowers and leaves to make greetings cards, bookmarks, or pieces of art.

—————— Continue adding vivid colours to this page.

350 ———————— Challenging yourself creatively can help take your mind off worries. Choose a colour and draw as many objects as you can that are that colour.

351

You can use art to tell stories, and stories can be found everywhere!
Visit a café or park and observe. Listen to what people say and look for
things that you find funny or interesting. Draw what you see or make notes.

*This little dog was on the floor
while her owner had lunch. She
wasn't happy with the situation.*

So she barked a lot.

*Then she was promoted to
prime position, not only on
her owner's lap but also in
easy reach of her owner's
lunch! It made me laugh.*

*Los Feliz,
Los Angeles, United States.*

352 ———— Draw a friend or family member, observing them from life.

353 ———— Using these marks as a starting point, create a piece of art.

354 ———— Draw all your favourite small objects. They could be trinkets, everyday items that you use or food that you like. Perhaps add a brightly coloured background behind them once you've finished.

355 ——— Colour.

356 ——— Your art can be inspired by absolutely anything. It doesn't need to be a traditional art subject, and it can be something very everyday. Draw some objects here that you find beautiful.

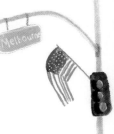

A lemon that
looks like a pear!

A strawberry
that looks
like an apple!

358

Lie on your front, on some grass, or on a mat or blanket. Take advantage of this new perspective and draw something you can see on the ground. Look out for things you haven't spotted before, such as unexpected patterns, details or colours.

359 —————— Make a piece of art where you focus on drawing the *negative space* rather than the subject itself. Negative space is the shape you can see around an object.

Tip: You could sketch out your subject very lightly in pencil first, and then erase it once you've finished.

Make abstract cards for your loved ones.

Start by gathering your materials. You'll need paint and paint brushes, some thin card, scissors, some pastels or coloured pencils and PVA glue. You'll also need some envelopes and stamps if you plan to send your cards.

Tip: Choose colours that go together nicely.

Paint a few of your pieces of thin card. Be confident with your mark-making. Drip paint, mix colours, and make quick strokes.

Tip: You could use some colours more than others.

While the painted thin card dries, use fresh sheets to make your blank cards. Fold each piece in half. You may want to trim your sheets beforehand, so that your cards will fit into small envelopes.

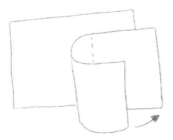

Once your painted card is completely dry, cut it up into smaller pieces. These could be loosely rectangular, or you may like to create curved shapes. It's up to you.

Tip: Make sure your cut pieces are small enough to fit onto your folded blank cards.

You may like to add some more detail to your little abstracts at this stage. Perhaps use oil pastel or coloured pencil to add lines and shapes.

Tip: If you use pastels, you can spray a fixative on top to prevent them from smudging.

Finally, stick each mini painting down onto the front of one of your folded blank cards. Use a thin layer of PVA glue or a gluestick.

Tip: To make sure they dry flat, put the cards under heavy books after you've stuck them down.
Insert a plain piece of paper either side of the cards when you do this so they don't get stuck to the book or each other!

Each card is its own little abstract masterpiece, so don't forget to give or send them! You could save them for special occasions, thank yous, or just send them to say hello!

Add in a beautiful sky. Perhaps there is a sunset, or lots of clouds?

362 ———————— Design a book cover for a book that you'd love to read.

363 ———— Design an empowering poster using a quote that inspires you.

364 ——————— Create a colourful mess!

365

Take some time to review your creative journey. Consider how art has made you feel happier, and write down any notes to remind yourself of things that you enjoy. You could also add drawings, and perhaps some notes on what you'd like to do next with your creativity!

Notes and ideas

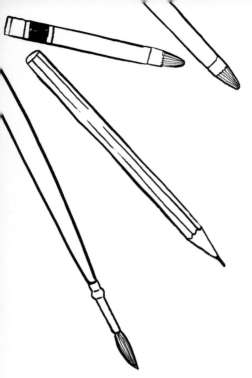

About the Author

Lorna Scobie grew up in the English countryside, climbing trees and taking her rabbit for walks in the fields. She is an author, illustrator and designer who is now based in south London. Growing up surrounded by nature has influenced her illustrations greatly, and her work often revolves around the natural world and animal kingdom.

Lorna always has a sketchbook close to hand when she's out and about, just in case. She enjoys spontaneity and the 'happy mistakes' that can happen along the way. Her favourite places to draw are museums, parks and botanical gardens.

This is the fifth book in Lorna's *365 Days* series, following on from *365 Days of Art*, *365 Days of Drawing*, *365 Days of Creativity* and *365 Days of Art in Nature*.

If you'd like to keep up to date with Lorna's work, she can be found on Instagram and Twitter: **@lornascobie**

www.lornascobie.com

Thank you

To Tom, always. And thank you also to my ever supportive and creative family, and my super editors, Kajal and Chelsea.

Quadrille, Penguin Random House UK, One Embassy Gardens, 8 Viaduct Gardens, London SW11 7BW

Quadrille Publishing Limited is part of the Penguin Random House group of companies whose addresses can be found at global.penguinrandomhouse.com

Published by Quadrille in 2022

www.penguin.co.uk

A CIP catalogue record for this book is available from the British Library

ISBN 978-1-78488-561-8
10 9 8

Publishing Director: Kajal Mistry
Senior Editor: Chelsea Edwards
Copy Editor: Jessica Spencer
Proofreader: Gaynor Sermon

Colour Reproduction by p2d

Printed and bound in China by C&C Offset Printing Co., Ltd.

The authorised representative in the EEA is Penguin Random House Ireland, Morrison Chambers, 32 Nassau Street, Dublin D02 YH68.

Penguin Random House is committed to a sustainable future for our business, our readers and our planet. This book is made from Forest Stewardship Council® certified paper.